MOTIVATIONAL MONDAY VITAMIN

WEEKLY SUB DIGEST

ADRIAN G. BUTLER, MBA

authorHOUSE®

AuthorHouse™
1663 Liberty Drive
Bloomington, IN 47403
www.authorhouse.com
Phone: 833-262-8899

Published by AuthorHouse 11/14/2023

ISBN: 979-8-8230-1245-4 (sc)
ISBN: 979-8-8230-1244-7 (e)

Library of Congress Control Number: 2023914190

Print information available on the last page.

FOREWORD

MOTIVATIONAL MONDAY VITAMIN INTRO

Everyone has a new beginning at some point in life, whether starting a new job, business, or family. In this small motivational read, that is exactly what you're getting- Newness! I'll preface this by first saying motivational literature have probably been around longer than some of us been alive in all different forms to a degree. Our educational institutions, historians, religious leaders, pioneers, mentors, favorite actor/s, sports stars, and modern-day fitness trainers-entrepreneurs are very inspirational, and in a lot of ways, motivational. This motivational read simply take you through a week-by-week basis of critical thinking and practical living. You'll see the weekly topic or in this case, vitamin that offers insight, wisdom, and key essential motivational strategies. Think of it as your weekly digest. Depending on your beliefs, core values, and spiritual faith, it's up to you to believe whether you're more than just a physical body. Most of us are aware we're made up of mind, body, and soul! Therefore, we need to feed our mind and soul as well as our bodies for continual growth and empowerment!

As author and founder of Motivational Monday Vitamin, the plan is to give wise insight, sound judgement, and tips of critical thinking for practical living while growing in the process. Born in Sumter, SC in 1977 as the fourth youngest of five children to two Philadelphia native African American parents. Times were tough as they struggled to make ends meet for a family of seven, but always provided food, shelter, discipline, and love. I grew up in an era where family core values were essential but not always cherished. In other words, as children hearing your parents give wise advice, strict discipline, admonition, and affirmation, you almost wish more of what was said could be seen or put into action to truly grasp the message.

Let me be the first to admit that I'm truly grateful for two living parents until this present day! Although they had their ups and downs while trying to make the family relationship work, they eventually separated and divorced in our critical years of on-set teenage development. As so many of our peers who grew up in broken or single-parent homes, we were right there along with them. Even in the midst of all the chaos, differences, confusion, resentment, pain, and turmoil, I witnessed something most single-parent homes wish they had, *parental resiliency.* Our parents may have had their differences while separated, but remained mutual friends to help raise us right and to the best of their ability. Honorable mention to my mother for gaining the strength and fortitude during the crucial moments of holding it down as a single parent!

I've gained the wisdom, ethos, grit, and determination from my parents in retrospect to my childhood. Now with a M.B.A in digital entrepreneurship with a thorough background in business, art, and fitness, it inspires me to fulfill my sole responsibility to three teenage children on their own journey! I realize no one is perfect as we all have flaws. However, I also understand mistakes can be repeated or simply resolved. Furthermore, I just want to suggest that no matter the detriment of the past, we are in control of changing the narrative. The Motivational Monday Vitamin sets the tone in giving you a voice and choice to make each day! Click your seat belts. You're now about to begin an exciting journey to empowering success!

Author- Adrian G. Butler

WEEK 1

MOTIVATIONAL MONDAY VITAMIN

(ENDURANCE)

As Americans living in the land of the "free," and "home of the brave," we are used to a certain norm in everyday life. Most of us have homes, cars, jobs, bank accounts, family, and friends. It seems like the more life evolves, the more we get accustomed to a microwavable society. Think about it, as the melting pot on God's green earth, we have access to just about everything at the tip of our fingers. The click of a mouse for tons of information, on demand delivery systems such as Amazon, Uber/ Lyft, Door Dash, etc. are just a few of many technologies satisfying our gratification! We're moving more towards an evolution of AI (Artificial Intelligence) with the autonomy of self-driven vehicles, robotics, climate globalization and human cyclones. The beauty of humanity is that it's always evolving and becoming more intelligent with technology from century to century. The motivational question of the week is "what are you waiting to happen next?" Whatever your expectations, the essential key take away is endurance!

Today's motivational vitamin is *endurance,* which is the power to bear through pain or difficult situations. We all wish at times through the snap of our fingers, things we long for could be fulfilled. Unfortunately, we know reality tells us that's seldom the case. Are you like so many others hoping and wishing things would happen instantaneously such as hitting the jackpot lottery or paying off a lump sum of debt? What about that family member or friend in a bad spot and can't wait for them to get themselves together? Is there a business on the radar, you can't wait to take off? Are you patient enough to endure through all the turmoil that it takes to get you there? We all heard patience is a "virtue." We need to remember endurance over instant gratification is a testament of how we live and view things in the world.

As you face the rest of the week and maybe can't wait until the weekend or next Monday for following segment in this book for whatever reason, my suggestion is continue reading until you feel like you need to stop. That in itself is a practical way of exercising endurance my friend! You do what you have to do to make the most of every opportunity and moment. If your back is against the wall with piles of work, deadlines, and mixed emotions, in a perfect world I would say to hit the Staples easy button. However, reality says to follow the Nike motto- "Just do it." If you just do it and endure the circumstances no matter how tough it gets, you'll find out genuine growth takes place much like a person going to gym, exercising while putting their muscles under strenuous stress.

WEEK 2

MOTIVATIONAL MONDAY VITAMIN

(HOPE)

Many people are waiting in eager expectation for things to happen or come about on a daily basis. Sometimes it seems difficult or discouraging when those same expectations are not met within our time frame. Who wants to wait around without any certainty of believing the expectations are going to come into fruition. Today's motivation Monday vitamin is *hope,* which is a feeling of expectation and desire for a certain thing to happen.

Hope is a foundational piece of who we are and why we believe what we believe. We hope for a lot of things because we're hopeful beings. You often hear individuals who commit crime and have no regards for human life are in need of hope! You can either be the recipient or constituent of hope. What are you hoping for today? Is it more money, more peace, love, creature comforts, self-esteem? Whatever your expectations, you can and will achieve it with a little bit of hope. Hope says to keep pressing when the tough gets going and the crap hits the fan. Everyone no matter their disposition need hope at some point in their lives.

Take a moment and reflect how hope operates on a day-to-day basis. Unfortunately, in a lot of uncertain situations, we flip the switch from despair to hope. When things appear gloomy like walking in a pitch dark room, we hope for some form of light to help guide us in the process. Most of us would begin praying if a loved one is suddenly in a life or death circumstance. Therefore, considering what you believe, prayer is a source of hope. When we get behind the wheel, we don't expect to get into any accident. However, we understand accidents do happen as we can only hope we make it back home in one peace. We hope our children or spouses don't disappoint us by taking wrong pathways and being disloyal. Therefore, hope is all about belief in something or someone we ultimately want to put our trust in.

Put it this way, without hope we're lost and without a sense of dignity. It's important to have hope in order to look forward to something we want to whole-heartedly believe! How about the hope the rest of this weekly digest meets your expectation and then some! Even if you're having a hard time grasping the idea of hope, you're not alone. It's really about facing your greatest fear. First, identify your fear.

Second, realize your fear is only as real as you make it out to be. Would you run from the shadow on the wall appearing to be bigger than the actual object it reflects? The answer determines how you perceive your circumstances surrounding you. Finally, after recognizing your fear for what it is, take an authoritative approach. This means taking the initiative to act with responsibility and accountability of hope. Remember to hold to each and every anticipated expectation as the benefits of it will serve you well when keeping it all in perspective.

MOTIVATIONAL MONDAY VITAMIN

(INTELLIGENCE)

There's so much philosophy and theoretical views surfacing in our modern-day world, that it seems complicated to decipher at times what are facts versus opinions. The media hype and prestigious iconic individuals are sharing while the entire world is listening. We tend to listen to people and sources that has credibility as well as impactful influences. However, what if that model-citizen who you look up to tends to go off on the deep in, doing or saying something absolutely devastating. Does that cause a change of perception for that person? Sure it does, based upon the extent of what transpired. That same person whether in media, politics, or sports are where they are due to having a level of intelligence that got them to their place of success!

Intelligence is more than just a word that should be thrown around lightly. Intelligence is defined as the ability to acquire and apply knowledge and skills. The question of the day is what are you using your intelligence for? Do you anticipate becoming more than ordinary to extraordinary? Do you aspire to change the world? How about being the next model-citizen, an iconic legend, or the next public political leader? Whatever it is we're trying to do or be in life, it will require using some intelligence to go to the next level. Remember it don't necessarily mean you have to be great for reaching the level of intelligence you're trying to achieve. It just means using your intelligence in a great way!

This is a nugget of truth for you to keep going, pushing, and willing yourself to that finish line of greatness. You do this by out-smarting your opponents with innovation, thinking outside the box with key concepts, separating yourself while creating wiggle room for the latest cutting edge of creativity. We learn from each other as our biggest assets. Don't be afraid to ask your neighbor or person you admire how they applied the knowledge they have to obtain the luxurious things you only wish you could obtain as well. Remember, knowledge is power! However, power is useless unless it's put to work. Don't just obtain knowledge and store it up all for yourself. Share it and apply what you know to impact the world at large!

WEEK 

MOTIVATIONAL MONDAY VITAMIN

(TIME)

In our busy world of planes, trains, and automobiles, the "Gig Economy" appears to be booming at its' peak. The unemployment rate currently sits at 3.6 percent with about 6 million people out of work. However, there appears to be only 1.7 million unemployment claims as of April 2022. That says one of two things, people are surviving on the income of loved ones, retirement, or they found another way of making money via start up business or the gig economy (i.e. shared rides transportation, door dash, Amazon, etc.). Whatever the rhyme and reason behind people working or choosing to be unemployed, there's always a motive to feel comfortable. We all know there are workaholics and others who are too lazy to work. Our modern-day world creates a lot of opportunities for everyone to stay busy. However, opportunities don't mean anything if we don't have time to take hold of those moments.

Today's motivational Monday vitamin is *time.* Time is defined as the measurable period during which an action, process, or condition exists or continues. Most of us as humans don't have enough of what we know as time. Time is viable and so crucial that once it's gone, we can never get it back! What are you doing with time? We all know there are 24 hours in a day, seven days a week, and 365 days a year. Each second that ticks away turns into minutes. Each minute that tick away turn into hours. The hours turn into days and so on.

How are we managing time? Do you get the most out of your day once hanging up your hard hat from work? How about the time we spend with family and loved ones? Does work, money, bills, and trips take precedence over what really matters? Once time runs out and it will for all of us, will there be any regrets? Could you really look back on life and say, "wow I really used my time well," or "man I wish I had more time to finish that project or spend with that loved one." No matter the outcome, the time factor starts fresh each day. No matter what happened yesterday or last year, the only thing we can control is our today to look forward to our tomorrow!

As you begin preparing for the week, remember you have only seven days with approximately 168 hours before meeting back at this point in one week, just to do it all over again. Time move faster than you and I can blink. That's why it's so important to make use of time while it's here! If you plan to accomplish something in time like attaining a higher education, getting married, starting a family, a start-up business, a faith-based ministry, or even buying a piece of property, what's stopping you from getting started? Don't regret allowing time to pass you by while the world is eating large. Just exercise the principle of starting and simply doing instead of waiting to make a move. Sometimes our biggest blessings await us when we mitigate procrastination!

WEEK 5

MOTIVATIONAL MONDAY VITAMIN

(ABILITY)

We often go through life with a mundane perspective of habitual routines such as preparing for work, meeting with a client, scheduling a doctor visit, taking kids to school, paying bills, etc. We as human beings are usually creatures of comfort. We strive to attain the "American Dream." People are classified as either poor, middle class, or wealthy (rich). Whatever classifications or side of the track we grew up on, most people behave the way they were taught as a child!

There's usually a grit and strong determination to work hard despite the economic status if one comes from a poor background versus one who was born with a *silver spoon in mouth.* This is not to say wealthy people don't work hard or have a strong work ethic because they certainly do! However, sometimes the difference between the wealthy individuals are the cultural values they were taught growing up. One might save every nickel and dime for fear of losing more than he or she spends. On the flip side, another might spend and invest more liquid assets to attain even more. We all heard the slogan "you have to pay to play," or "it takes more to make more." Smart businesspeople understand it takes working capital to make any business successful. There needs to be a cash flow of more money coming in than going out (income-to-debt ratio) to make a profit.

Today's motivational vitamin is *ability.* One needs ability to accomplish any given task. It is defined as "the possession of the means or skill to do something." The very fact that you got up this morning, made it to work or class, ate breakfast, and somehow reading this serves as a uniqueness of having ability. In some cases, people are impaired or incapable in their natural ability to accomplish the same task we do without saying. We can open our eyes and see the beauty of life while unfortunately, there are blind individuals who can never sense that ability. We can independently brush our teeth, bathe, and dress in our own fashion while others who don't have limbs or capability of fine motor skills need full assistance.

Think about the ability you have each day oppose to focusing on your limitations in comparison to others. If all you know to do is working well with people, do it with confidence and expertise so that you're feeling good at the end of day! Whatever God-given talent and ability you have, it is imperative to use it without any limits. We might look at what we have as small but to others, it's huge and hold so much more weight than we can ever imagine. The next time someone asks you what you are naturally good at, there should be no hesitation or doubt if you have one functional brain, a caring heart, lungs to breathe, ten fingers & toes, and legs to walk.

MOTIVATIONAL MONDAY VITAMIN

(GROWTH)

Here we are in another week with a new day of opportunity and perseverance. Some of us struggled to get up out of bed this morning, hitting snooze button while others without second-guessing it routinely awoke with no struggle. We routinely conducted the things we usually do on Monday morning. We don't think twice about things we usually do like brushing our teeth, grooming our hair, bathing, dressing, eating, etc. The things that become surprising to us are the "uh oh" moments when situations begin to spiral out of control or we're suddenly facing a whole new set of circumstances. You might be driving to work and boom there's an accident that causes you to run late, or how about that sudden car maintenance leading to another unexpected repair bill. We all been there catching bad news in the least unexpected moments. It's devastating at times when facing tough circumstances. However, there's purpose behind the circumstance that normally leads to growth.

Today's motivational Monday vitamin is *growth.* Growth is defined as the act or process of growing; development; gradual increase in size. Growth is the measure of one's physical stature or character development. It really depends on how people view growth and its' significance. You would think a child who know they need to have a well-balanced diet filled with proteins, vegetables, and calcium like plenty of milk is obviously concerned with their physical growth. On the contrary, a child who normally does not eat vegetables or have a well-balanced meal is not concerned about their physical growth. It was the popular cultural norm for hearing ads in 80s & early 90s to "drink milk… it does a body good." We would see ads like Tony the Tiger in a frosted flake commercial saying "They're Grrreat." How about Michael Jordan who everyone wanted to emulate say "you better eat your Wheaties" in a Wheaties commercial.

There are many areas of growth beside the physical stature. We know people who are fitness buffs that will eat and train intensively for muscular growth. We know there are individuals who study hard in school to become doctors and lawyers. The principle is learning what causes growth. If anyone want to be good at anything, he or she must practice and work hard at their craft! No famous person became famous overnight. It took turmoil, hard work, and true dedication to make their dream come alive. Some people like to wear shiny jewelry as part of fashion & style! That same jewelry had to go through intensive heat, fire, fermentation as it melted and seem useless before it turned out to be very valuable! What are you willing to go through to shine, and create more value to you who are? Whatever it is, remember growth is always taking place as long as we bear up under the circumstances and learning from it as part of the journey in the process!

MOTIVATIONAL MONDAY VITAMIN

(VIGILANT)

Have you had your boost this morning? How many cups of coffee did you drink? Did you take your multivitamin along with breakfast this morning? Maybe you got up extra early and worked out at the gym before getting started with your day. You feel good now that your blood is circulating, and adrenaline has kicked in! Otherwise, you rolled over in bed this morning, hit the snooze on alarm clock and back to sleep you went. You soon realized whether getting up early or later, there was a purpose of getting up. You could've stayed in bed and wasted time away or made the decision you did in waking up to get started with the day! Remember, it's always a choice, a decision of freewill "to be or not to be," "to act or not react" in any given situation. In our world of social media and new ageism, informational news sources are moving at a high rapid pace. If we're not being proactive, more than likely we become reactive.

Today's motivational Monday vitamin is *vigilant,* which means keeping careful watch for possible danger or difficulties. Ever since the pandemic in 2020, most people gained a conscious awareness to be more proactive when it comes to their health and stocking up on necessities in the household. Most of us remember when the country and around the world was on locked down. Some people felt like prisoners in their own homes, becoming depressed while others unfortunately, committed suicide. We've never experienced anything like the magnitude of Covid-19 pandemic, with maybe the exception of the Spanish-Flu before some of our time. The survivors during those moments, which include people like yourself, and many others who remained vigilant to make it to this day! Otherwise, you don't get to this day without displaying a capacity of vigilance or bravery!

It's time to be more proactive, showing an even-kill of preparation with some heart to face the things we're facing today. It's so easy to complain and talk about the current events affecting us. However, the difficult part is trying to be part of the solution and saying to ourselves "how do I help this situation?" We need to go throughout this week and focus on how we get to safety rather than magnifying the danger. If we're in a burning building, we're taught to "stop, drop, and roll." If we're lost out on the deep sea while sinking, we need to wear our life jackets and signal for help. If the plane takes a nosedive, we need to follow directions with putting on oxygen mask before helping anyone else. If the drinking water and other necessities run out on the shelves at local stores due to a crisis, we need not panic but depend on each other. Remember to stay vigilant so that life could continue to carry you through the toughest of times!

WEEK 8

MOTIVATIONAL MONDAY VITAMIN

(CONSISTENCY)

What truly marks the character of a great person or what does it take to reach a status of greatness? Does it require being wishful and hoping greatness arise as a genie popping out of a bottle? How about blood, sweat, and tears with true grit and never giving up on your dreams? Whatever the purpose behind greatness, it will come at a cost. Many might assume greatness compares to one's socioeconomic status, power, or the many inspirational ways one leaves as an influential impact on the world. Others might dear believe being great is about how much you accomplished or even dominated as a human being.

We often wondered why people become raving fans of iconic stars like Michael Jackson, Teddy Pendergrass, Prince, Michael Jordan, Kobe Bryant, and yes, even Tom Brady to name a few. We all witnessed these fans hysterically crying, falling out, and almost worshipping some of these stars as if they were part of deity! The aura that's in the air resonates with the fans due to the dominating performance of their favorite stars' craft! These figures became bigger than life!

No matter the craft, ability, performance, or the person that exemplifies greatness, the beauty is in the eye of the beholder. In other words, we can all speculate what true greatness is by our perception. How do you perceive greatness? At the end of the day, greatness may have many different meanings. However, we need to dig deeper in what leads to greatness. Remember the popular saying "it's not how you start; it's how you finish." We all know we can't finish any task without being consistent throughout the process.

Today's motivational vitamin is *consistency.* Consistency is defined as an agreement or harmony of parts to one another or a whole. In other words, there's correspondence involved. We can never get to a status of greatness if we're being inconsistent. Those iconic public figures mentioned earlier carried a legacy of greatness because of their consistency. They did it day in and day out. Imagine having so much potential and skillful ability to work a craft or talent that is God-given and not exercising it. It would be an absolute devastation to not utilize something you know you're good at with a level of consistency. Life happens and sometimes become unfair when there's a fork in the road. A sudden natural disaster happens, health issues pop up, or we lose a loved one, causing our focus to shift or go down the wrong path. No matter the circumstances or how tough life gets, if we ever want to reach a level of greatness, we must be consistent in whatever we do daily!

WEEK 

MOTIVATIONAL MONDAY VITAMIN

(PURPOSE)

Here we are on another beautiful Monday morning or afternoon, where the birds are chirping, the sun is shining, the breeze is calmly blowing, and traffic is forever moving around the globe. Most of us woke up in our right state of mind while others took their final breath before sunrise. Our eyes beheld and ears heard all the tragic news that unfolded within the last 24-48 hours. People are waking up different than when they laid down last night. Some are awakening to terrible news of losing a loved one, while others to another chance at life! We often wonder why some of the current events unfold the way it does, leaving many of us in a state of shock.

We're living in a day and time where innocent bystanders are being unfortunately hurt or mistakenly killed over nonsense! We can't begin to live our lives in fear due to what's happening around us. However, there needs to be an opposite approach to operate in boldness. No matter what the state legislature decides upon on gun laws or Roe V. Wade, the ultimate power lies in our hand as citizens to make the change! True change can never occur if our mentality remains the same of carrying on with our daily lives, without a shift to impact others in need of support.

You might ask why should I have to ever shift my focus to influencing change when it doesn't directly affect me? Why put myself at risk for the sake of someone I don't know or affiliated with? What do I really get out of it or how does it impact the decisions I make? Purpose is all you need to know to answer every question or doubt that might come up. Purpose is defined as the reason for which something is done or created or for which something exists. The real questions should be why was I created?

What is my mission in life? What can I do more of that I'm good at? What is limiting myself from super exceeding expectations required of me? Whatever the purpose we are destined to fulfill, remember it will require making change for ourselves for the benefit of others. If you tend to procrastinate a lot or fiddle your thumbs when it comes to fulfilling your dreams, make a change to do something different one step at a time and watch how change come about!

MOTIVATIONAL MONDAY VITAMIN

(PROGRESS)

Life experiences is the best teacher surrounding our circumstances. We usually learn viable information when we subject ourselves to authority. For example, starting a new job position or running a franchise business for first time will require removing the hat of expertise and putting on the shoes of humility! In other words, we should never function as if we're experts in a new practice or field of study, when there's always room for growth! We need to remind ourselves to stay in the moment, not living beneath or beyond our means!

Today's motivational vitamin is *progress*, which means forward or onward movement toward a destination. It's relative to space and time. We need to make sure we're keeping ourselves in check for progress. How much progress was made between last year and this present day? How far did you reach in that particular goal? Some of us as parents witnessed our children making progress in obtaining driver's license, starting college, or adjusting behavior patterns for first time. If we look at our goals personified as babies, we understand there are phases in crawling before walking and babbling before talking. Otherwise, growth is necessary to reach a level of maturity and accomplishing goals no matter how small or big they are!

It goes without saying that most of us, if not all witnessed progress being made within the past couple of years post Covid-19. We certainly thought the sky was falling and the distinction of humanity was upon us during the huge pandemic scare in 2020. Somehow, our resilience as humans kicked in whether you want to call it survival mode or following protocol, we managed to figure it out via learned behavior. Remember, if we're not making moves forward, more than likely we become stagnant and start going backwards. When we think of anything electrifying going backwards, the "moonwalk" is what comes to mind. Otherwise, going backwards instead of forward don't seem like a lot of fun. Challenge yourself this week to make more progress so that you're one more step closer in attaining that goal than you were yesterday!

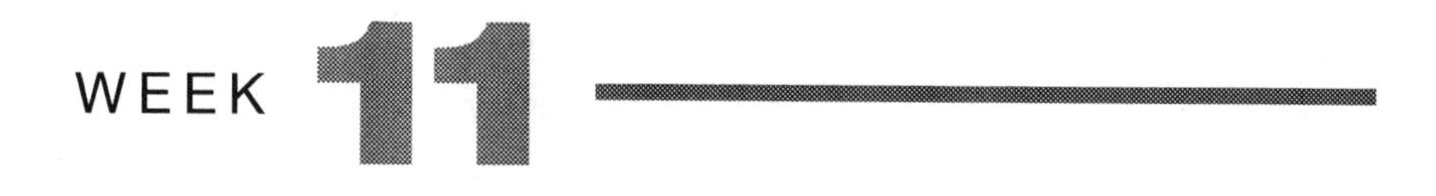

MOTIVATIONAL MONDAY VITAMIN

(PREPARATION)

No one really likes being caught off guard. Most people respond to surprises differently whether it's good or bad news. Think about it, our adrenaline gets flowing as we either go into fight or flight mode. We face challenges each day, hoping to rise above with resiliency and perseverance. We heard the famous quote "what doesn't break us will ultimately make us." On the flip side, "what doesn't make us will try to break us." The point is circumstances will either make us better when facing the challenges head on, or eventually break us if we do not respond well! The only way we can respond well is being ready when the bell rings. The indicator that determines if we tend to respond well or not is preparation.

Preparation is today's motivational vitamin, which is defined as the action or process of making ready. If the truth be told, we're never prepared or ready to hear bad news. On the contrary, we expect or motivate ourselves to hear good news even if there's any inclination of bad waiting in the shadows. When we're hit with sudden bad news about our health or loss of a loved one, are we really prepared? The answer is NO! Most of us have been in situations of losing our jobs at some point in life and not fully prepared when it happened. An unexpected bill popped up when we weren't prepared. A sudden ailment began wreaking havoc on our health without preparing us for it. We can't really prepare for what we are unable to control. However, preparation is our map or dashboard if you will that points out our destiny.

Preparation is the main essential component to success! Think of it as having water to drink or bathe with. Without it there's no hydration or purification which defeats the purpose to accomplish the task at hand. Preparation should be thought of as a compass in the hand of a camper on a long journey. You're never loss if you have the compass which gives you the wrong or right direction you're headed. We need to prepare ourselves for being better than we were yesterday. If we dropped the ball and feel like we were so close to reaching that goal, it's not too late! If you are breathing with another day to wake up, there's opportunity to prepare for whatever is in front of you. Never let excuses be the backdrop of why there was failure and no success. Prepare yourself for excellence today, so there's no regret for tomorrow.

MOTIVATIONAL MONDAY VITAMIN

(OPPORTUNITY)

The question we need to ask ourselves this morning is what kind of person do I want to be? Most of us know or have a pretty good feeling of who we are without saying. Are you satisfied with the person you've become or is there more room for growth? Do you see yourself on the outside looking in when good things seem to be happening to others? More importantly, how do you measure your self-worth? Do you take joy in what you do? Do you tend to think of yourself more highly than you should considering the position you're in? How about our confidence and self-esteem? Are we easily impacted or influenced by what others perceive about us? Do we feel less confident with low self-esteem based on our performance or the kind of work we do? These are just a few of many questions raised from a human emotional intelligence standpoint of who we are opposed to who we want to be!

The beauty of transformation is in the journey. In other words, we all have experiences that can make us or break us. There have been times we conducted ourselves in ways that seem honorable to others, while juggling with moments of failure and defeat! We all wish sometimes this was a perfect world where there was no such thing as hatred, bigotry, violence, or death. However, we know the very opposite is true, where we are sure to face these unfortunate circumstances as human beings accounting for only 0.01% of earth population. In the crucial moments we have on earth, we need to take advantage of every good opportunity as possible.

Today's motivational vitamin is *opportunity,* which means a set of circumstances that make it possible to do something. A question relating back to how we perceive ourselves should also include "Is it who I know or what I do that makes me into a better version of myself? One thing rest assured, opportunity allows us to make a decision whether we want to go from good to great, ordinary to extraordinary, average to excellent in all we plan do in life. If the truth is told, we all are looking for opportunities to become even better version of ourselves.

We should always remember, it's not so much in what we do that presents opportunity, but who we know and surround ourselves with that give opportunities. If you want to be great, surround yourself with great people. If there's opportunity to make more money, connect with sources who know how to be successful. Feeling depressed, or hopeless, seek out a therapist or surround yourself with people who are spiritual, upbeat, and positive! Do whatever it takes to create opportunity to get one step closer to where you want to be in life!

MOTIVATIONAL MONDAY VITAMIN

(PATIENCE)

Today's world is filled with all kinds of craziness, drama, heartache, adventure, and fun! We're ever evolving as a people, getting smarter throughout time. The beauty of humanity is the realism of bringing things to life! By nature, we are innovators, creators, philanthropists, scientists, motivators, shakers, and movers just trying to contribute to the "American Dream." We've come so far as a nation and have so much more room for growth. Technology has shifted to a new paradigm since the start of the 21st century. We're now moving more towards the new era of robotics and artificial intelligence. Have you ever noticed how things are getting faster as we move with time? Heck, the more we age, the faster it seems like life is on a rapid pace. We try to get more accomplished, set additional goals, become wiser, spend more time with family, and have plenty of fun. Some would even say we live in a microwavable society where we want things at our fingertips for instant gratification.

The values we normally display usually come from our upbringing. We know how to complete home-based skills like personal hygiene, cooking, cleaning, and dressing appropriately from the discipline of our parents or guardians. In some cases, we would hear them say things like "just wait… be patient," "don't be in a rush to be grown," etc. Today's motivational vitamin is Patience which means to accept or tolerate delay, trouble, or suffering without getting upset/angry.

Most of us going throughout the rest of this week will need to exercise patience. We're faced with so many obstacles regarding work, school, family, traffic, finances, and health concerns to name a few. We heard the old saying "Good things come to those who wait." We know patience is a virtue because it's something we train ourselves to have. Our first reaction when someone cuts us off the road or acts impatiently rude towards us, is to get upset or angry. We can either respond by getting on their level with a similar reaction or we can choose the higher road with exercising patience!

We need to have patience when it comes to responding to circumstances and waiting for our current situation to change. We can't and will not get anywhere significant in life by cheating ourselves. Think of patience as a beautiful plant that you want yourself to resemble. It can only flourish, remain stable with vibrancy and attraction if proper nutrients, sun light, water, and care allows it to do so. We determine whether we want to resemble always being in a hurry, stumbling along the way, or having patience so that growth is taking place for our future!

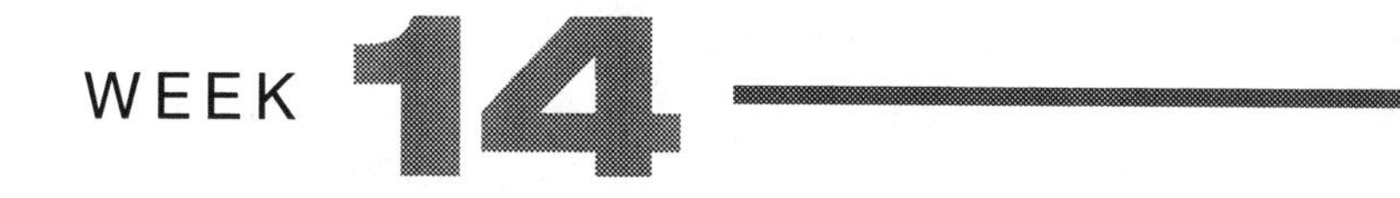

MOTIVATIONAL MONDAY VITAMIN

(CONTROL)

Are you conscious of the world around you? Do things seem promising or gloomy? Are the skies falling or do you have a glimpse of hope? Whatever the situation there must be a reality check instead of looking at things with a half-glass-full approach. Life is unpredictable at times because we never know what each day will bring. We can only live our lives the best way we can by faith, trust, guidance, and morale! Most people live according to standards, rules, principles, and governing laws. We know wars tend to break out when there seem to be a small break in these principles. Dictatorship and anarchy begin to arise when there's no set of rules in place. Imagine if we didn't have rules or guiding principles in our homes like cleaning up between meals, flushing toilet with proper etiquette, following directions, or removing shoes upon entry into homes, etc. It would be an absolute crazy zone filled with chaos because something would be lacking. Common sense tells us we need to abide by authorities to keep us safe and under control.

Today's motivational Monday vitamin is *control,* which means the power to influence or direct people's behavior or the course of events. If you're human, it's common to want some form of control. It starts in childhood, gaining a sense of independence and continues into adulthood, even old age. We want to stir the wheel at times on the ship of life with no co-pilots in sight. Sometimes it's flat out dangerous to have control especially when there's fear of the unknown. In other words, we need to leave some things up to the authorities and experts to handle while exercising a little more patience.

Most of us understand there's good and bad to having control! It's good to be in control of our household, raising children, paying bills, and providing wholesomeness. It's a good thing to have control of our temper when upset or angry, not overly reacting in our emotions. On the flip side, it's bad to lose control of our emotions that could possibly lead to devastation! It happens all the time in our today's world. Road rage and murder retaliation leading to more killings. Homicides and robberies have gone up dramatically due to a lack of self-control.

We must go through this week understanding if we ever want to get somewhere significant in life, there must be a level of control. We can't be afraid to allow others in authority to have a form of control for sake of maintaining order in the world. Sometimes we must stop trying to control something that is out of our control. Work on things we know we can control like adjusting our attitude, choice of words, awareness, and respect to peers and authorities. We need to know when to be in control versus allowing life to have full control when facing adversity. Control what you can control and leave the rest up to trust, divine intervention and guidance!

MOTIVATIONAL MONDAY VITAMIN

(APPRECIATION)

Ask yourself this question, am I naturally a taker or giver? The best way to determine the answer to that question is asking yourself what gives me more fulfillment when giving or receiving? If you take a piece of paper and begin jotting down all the things you love to receive versus giving away, what will outweigh the other? Before I go any further, I should preface this by saying there's nothing wrong with giving or receiving. In fact, it's a blessing in both aspects when we give and receive. The issue may be when one is always giving and never makes room to receive in return, or when one is always receiving but never seem to give in return.

There should be a balance when it comes to both aspects of giving and receiving so one don't seem like it's outweighing the other. Most people want nice things that we can relate to as part of our creature comforts: immaculate homes, luxury cars, high-paying careers, stable relationships, etc. How many of us are willing to share these creature comforts with others? Are we willing to make sacrifices so that others could have these luxuries well after we are dead and gone? Do we accept and receive blessings for ourselves only with no intent to give back?

Whatever our motive when it comes to giving and receiving, we cannot overlook the appreciation it takes to give any credence! Today's motivation Monday vitamin is *appreciation,* which is a feeling or expression of admiration, approval, or gratitude. The next time someone does a favor on your behalf, instead of saying "Thank you," express it by going a little deeper. Switch up the wording and say, "I appreciate you!" If your texting, give some emojis in expressive form to make the person feel special in return. Someone shares something very knowledgeable to you so that you can ultimately share it with others. Remember, our true selves come out when something is given to us or when we do for others. We can either share in some way or another what was given or keep it all to ourselves.

Bottom line, always show appreciation by being appreciated! We can never fully understand what appreciation is until actively expressing it, giving it, and receiving it. Go throughout the rest of this week with a true appreciation that for one, you woke up this morning. Two, you're in your right mind. Third, there's family and friends who loves you dearly! Remember, appreciation is bigger than you and I. It has everything to do with expression of internal gratitude! It's not just lip service. It's saying I will express my deepest emotion of gratitude towards you so that you can sense the genuine authenticity rather than just words.

WEEK 16

MOTIVATIONAL MONDAY VITAMIN

(REMEMBER)

This morning, we're cutting right to the chase. Our Motivational Monday vitamin is *remember,* which means to have in or be able to bring to one's mind an awareness of someone or something that has seen, known, or experienced in the past. Today is a day to reflect, remember, recall, and recite all of life's memories. We take pride in our accomplishments, achievements, and goals as we should! However, let us never forget what it took to get us there.

The ultimate sacrifices of family and friends watching the little ones while you sat in class or studied for exams. How about the spouse who held it down at home while you put in major hours to move it up in the ranks at work or attain that credentialing license? Remember the personal encounter with that stranger that ultimately took a chance on you and gave you more than an opportunity. Don't forget about our ancestors who delicately helped pave the way to this country. The point is no matter where you find yourself in life, our memory banks should be full of recollection to keep us in check!

Always remember that it is a true gift to utilize our memory exercised as part of the central nervous system. Our brains function as the operating station of what we think, how we feel, and next move we will make. It is by far the strongest muscle in the human body! There are people who take daily supplements to maintain a healthy brain function. There are those who are constantly reminded by family and circle of support what life was once like as they can no longer remember because of brain trauma or cognitive dysfunction.

Life will sometimes become discouraging to most of us in some form or another. Whether a loss of a job, a loved one, health, or financial stability, that is where we remind ourselves if we survived it before we can survive it again! Life is all about making memories if you really think about it. It is what we do in the here and now with our loved ones that matter. Make a difference in this world so that you can be part of change! Be more than just ordinary, be great! Set a legacy like the trailblazers of old and be remembered for more of what you can offer rather than who you can be!

MOTIVATIONAL MONDAY VITAMIN (CONFIDENCE)

We begin this day on the strength in knowing our daily routine will be accomplished without any disruption! Most of us get up thinking what we will wear, what to fix for breakfast, the time preparation for work, and what we will take out to eat later for dinner. No matter the activity, the bottom line is we try to figure out if there's any distractions or anything surprisingly scheduled that will perhaps take away time from our daily routine. The moment distractions or alterations in schedule appear, we immediately begin thinking how we're going to accomplish the original task at hand. The good news is that we normally figure it out, even if our regularly scheduled activity is delayed or sacrificed for the sake of another purpose. There's no sense for being weak-minded or caving into the pressure of our own self-centered will when our routine is interrupted. There needs to be a confidence that whatever happen in a typical day, there is an ultimate purpose behind what just interrupted our schedule.

Today's motivational vitamin is *confidence,* which means feeling sure of yourself, or someone or something, firm trust. It means having a certainty of your abilities. Therefore, no matter the distractions with an unexpected, surprising phone call, a sudden health concern, or even a past due hefty bill, confidence says be calm and trust the process! We heard the saying "there's no use in crying over spilled milk." The meaning behind it is an accident occurred, now it's time to clean it up or do something about it. Most circumstances happen with a particular purpose in mind. Growth! Therefore, we can never fully experience character growth if there's no confidence or if it's lacking in a certain area.

Confidence says that I'm going to be the best at this no matter how many times I fail or struggle to get it right! It's being sure that whatever you're trying to accomplish will get done with maximum effort and fortitude. How are you ever going to accomplish the goal you started without having confidence? How are you going to achieve that dream job without looking the employer in the eyes and having confidence? How are you going to begin the path of articulating your words with fluency and communicating more efficiently without confidence? Confidence is a powerful weapon and if used correctly will silence the doubters, kill the haters, and brighten the darkness.

We need to remind ourselves- to get from Monday to Friday, confidence is the driving force that will help aid in getting us there! It would be like leaving home without your car keys. How are we getting to our destination without the key essential tool to help drive us there? Always have confidence when it seems like the world is crumbling around you so that you end up on the safer side when all the smoke has cleared.

MOTIVATIONAL MONDAY VITAMIN

(LISTEN)

Good morning! A friendly greeting can never hurt as you prepare to take another weekly dose of the Motivational Monday Vitamin. How are you feeling this morning? Are you off on a good start or are things unfortunately spinning out of control before you could put a finger to it? Ask yourself am I excited and glad to be alive to see another day or am I just going through the motions in the land of the living? Whatever feelings you have right now should be one of gratitude that you opened your eyes, able to see while breathing and warm blood flowing through your veins.

How do you perceive yourself versus the world around you? Do you feel confident or inadequate based on your skill set or level of competition you're up against? What are your views on life and creation? Do you walk with purpose every day, or do you feel like life has become burdensome with unfortunate circumstances and loss? Our emotional intelligence tends to shift our thinking and perception about things in a totally different light. In other words, we come to a mutual understanding of what others are going through and what's happening in the world around us.

Therefore, as we get started with today, we need take the focus off ourselves and shed some compassion on people in much worse circumstances. The only way we can take the focus off ourselves for just a little bit and be of genuine impact is blocking out the noise with a new method of thinking. The essential way we can begin to block out the noise is starting to listen. Today's Motivational Monday Vitamin is "listen," which means to give one's attention to sound; make effort to hear something. How often do you talk versus listening? To listen is to hear, which mean you're paying attention to gain understanding. There's a golden adage you might've heard stating "we were given two ears and one mouth to listen twice as much as we talk." Think about it, the human anatomy is wired to listen and see twice as much than it speaks. In today's world, most people want to do twice more talking than listening which makes it unbearable to understand others.

Bottom line, we need to practice the skill of listening so that we never rush to judgement about someone or something. If you ever sat and just listened to someone going through crisis or experiencing a bad day, that individual more than likely will share an incredible appreciation of you for doing so! Listening is a viable part of therapy for self and others. Nothing frustrates a parent more than their own child who don't listen. In fact, it shows a level of disrespect of one choosing to ignore something knowing concise instruction was given. Therefore, as we go throughout this week, we should train our minds to listen more than we speak. One who is wise is one who listens. One who listens is one who have understanding.

MOTIVATIONAL MONDAY VITAMIN

(JOURNEY)

Things don't always end the way they started. Think about the last time you began doing something, whether it was starting a business, writing a book, enrolling in a class, or joining an intense workout program. What was the outcome? How did you feel when you first started that project or latest invention versus how you feel about it now? Remember that feeling of being on cloud nine and so adamant about your decision-making? That perception, "I got this and nothing is getting in my way!" We know realistically that it takes time to achieve goals and reach the pinnacle of success in whatever we attempt to do. However, we have to remind ourselves that success is not so much about the outcome, but the journey!

Today's Motivational Monday vitamin is *journey,* which is an act of traveling from one place to another. Believe it or not, everyone in life is on a journey! Most people probably don't look at life as a journey. It's not until you can begin to see life experiences from different lenses that ultimately will shift your way of thinking. When you think of journey, what do you normally envision? A trip somewhere? A process of becoming? Maybe a marathon race? Understand a journey is what you make it out to be. You don't necessarily have to take a long trip somewhere to be on a journey. A journey always starts and ends with you telling your story. How do you want people to remember your story when it ends? We all love a good story and even better when it has a happy ending! Rarely do anyone enjoy a movie with an exciting beginning but sad ending.

Always remember to end the journey with a happy ending. It will only end up being boring or sad if you allow it to. Control the things you can control and leave the rest up to the creator of your soul to do the rest! Some journeys are long while others are short. You play a major role in how that journey begins and ends! Let this week be the week you pick up the pieces where you last left off for accomplishing your dream. It's about the ups and downs and circumstances you had to endure to get to where you are. It's the ride on the way to the moon or your place of destiny. When you finally reach that goal or level of success, count your blessings and understand the real blessing is in the journey!

WEEK 20

MOTIVATIONAL MONDAY VITAMIN

(CARE)

Has it ever occurred to you that every time you turn on the television to watch the local or worldwide news, you hear more about bad things than the good? There seems to be an overwhelming domination of bad news seeping through the tubes with a particular purpose in mind. It's meant to grab our attention. This is how the major anchor channel networks make their bread and butter by attracting viewership! If you ever noticed how the news programming is structured to immediately grab people attention, the first thing you usually see is the most exciting or depressed, alarming news. The producers figure a great proportion of viewers will tune in during the most opportunistic time. Unfortunately, the attention grabber seeks to draw in viewers while exposing sometimes tragic news.

There are urban communities labeled as hot zones with deadly shootings and homicides on the rise. The problem is with some of the bad news of neighborhood homicides and massive shootings, it becomes a sad song that no one wants to hear any more. The local media coverage run it every day because they know a ton of people are going to watch it every day. No discredit to the news channel networks only doing their job and keeping viewers informed. However, it must come a time when even the networks say enough is enough with the same sad song! It's okay to inform the public of tragic news, but it truly needs to be a balance in switching things up. So many people have become desensitized by the same unfortunate tragedies of gun violence that they're turned away from some of the sources giving it.

Today's motivational Monday vitamin is *care,* which means watchful or protective attention, caution, concern, or regard usually towards an action or situation. We're living in a time where it seems most people don't care how much you know until they know how much you care! A student will respect a teacher more when there's a true concern for his or her growth oppose to an instructor that can care less. You're either growing in hatred or growing in love, bottom line. Again, we become desensitized as there is a lack of care for our surrounding neighbors or world at large when tragedy is not directly knocking at our front door. Just because the tragedy is not happening to you or people you know, doesn't mean you should not care! We need to first care for ourselves and for each other to make this world a better place.

You might ask why should I care for people and unfortunate circumstances that are not directly impacting me? Would those same individuals care for me if facing a similar crisis? Again, remember you're either part of the problem or a solution willing to fix the problem. Don't allow deception or philosophy to dictate your character as a human being. We must step up to the plate and begin to give to the needy on the street, spread words of encouragement among the discouraged, love the unlovable, get out our own way and find ways to care for others.

WEEK 21

MOTIVATIONAL MONDAY VITAMIN

(ALERT)

Here we go, it's Monday again! The beginning of a new work week for some while it's a never-ending story for others. Were you looking forward to seeing this day? Did you somehow catch the jitterbug or become suddenly nervous? Did you know studies suggests the risk of a heart attack increases by 20% on Monday, more than any other day of the week? Whether that philosophy is true or not, it's got to be something to stressors on Mondays, causing a toll on our health. Ask yourself "do I really like what I do?" Do I get fulfillment out of my everyday duties so much so, that I'm looking forward to the following week? Are distractions or plain ole procrastination eating up most of my time that it prevents me from being productive?

Whatever the answers to those questions, we need to pinpoint the motive that is driving us to success. Is it more lucrative money? Is it purpose and fulfillment? Is it just getting by and being comfortable? If Mondays or preparing for a new week is a challenge, it's probably best to try doing something different.

The only way we can try something different is having clarity with a change of mind mentality. If things seem cloudy and gloomy while attempting to reach your goals, it doesn't always necessarily mean you're doing something wrong. It could just mean distractions are set up in your path like hurdles in a 1500 sprint. If you're not aware of the hurdles in the race, thinking it is just a sprint to the finish line, then you're in for a rude awakening. You must realize for any pathway to success, it causes less focus on distractions and more attention to alertness.

Today's motivational Monday vitamin is *alert,* which is defined as a state of careful watching and readiness especially for danger or opportunity. To be alert means being careful of your surroundings. To know what being alert looks like, we must do a little digging. Does it mean we're constantly looking over our shoulders when out in the public? Does it mean having 24/7 video surveillance? Does it require having phone settings in emergency mode? How about staying focus with the task at hand? Most people probably would think it's eliminating distractions. Well, there is no wrong answer to these questions. In fact, doing all these things is essential to being alert.

Bottom line, we need to go throughout this week reminding ourselves to be vigilant, staying on guard, and watchful while minimizing distractions. If that means not holding phone in hand while texting and driving, that's what it means. If it requires checking door ring surveillance every so often for any suspicious activity, go for it! Maybe you want to have your phone on speed dial for 911 or emergency contact in case of a dangerous situation. Have a mindset to defend yourself by any means should you face a vulnerable encounter with someone. We never want to overreact in any given situation. The best thing to do is stay calm and act alert!

WEEK 22

MOTIVATIONAL MONDAY VITAMIN

(DISCIPLINE)

Who says you can't be more than who you're destined to be? Why do we tend to feed our mind with deceptive lies about restricted limitations and unrealistic expectations? Are you afraid to fail? News flash, if you never fail, do you know what it's really like to succeed? The point is as humans we learn to crawl before we walk. In the process of learning to walk, we stumble and fall along the way as part of the process. No millionaire or even billionaire comes out the womb with money in their hand. Some might inherit wealth, but still need to know how to manage it to be successful. What will it take to get beyond our ultimate doubts and fears? Is it living in the shadow of our gritty friends and family? Is it taking on more responsibility to prove confidence? No matter how deep you dig for answers, it will require discipline to put it plainly.

Today's motivational Monday vitamin is *discipline,* which means to punish or penalize for sake of enforcing obedience and perfecting moral character. It has a strong reference of making something correct by inflicting a level of pain. As parents, we know how to discipline our children with a hopeful expectation that they learn from their mistakes and don't repeat it. A pro athlete knows how to discipline his or her body for workout, diet, and sleeping habits to perform at their highest level. Most working-class citizens know how to discipline themselves to be at work on time or at the very least, show up for sake of not losing their jobs.

Discipline should not be taken lightly nor thought of as a curse word. On the contrary, it should be thought of as a blessing in disguise! It's like medicine for our ultimate pain pressure points. If you don't learn to discipline yourself, it would be very difficult to digest anything like this vitamin and begin applying it for daily practical living. We must wake up each morning with discipline in mind. We need discipline to not indulge in sweets, alcohol, or things that can cause chronic health problems. We must discipline ourselves for greatness even when the odds are against us. As an inspiring writer and motivator, I must discipline myself on a weekly basis to create the next motivational vitamin despite my urges to watch sports or favorite TV series. I realize the end goal benefits my viewers more than it would ever benefit me as the author.

Bottom line, take pride in discipline the next time you're corrected by your supervisor, parent, or person of authority. It only means that person giving the correction or discipline wants to see growth and progress! We can never grow or reach our destiny in life without discipline. Sometimes we must discipline ourselves to see the highest potential that no one else can see. Discipline is a lifelong journey. Are you willing to be part of that journey, where it gets hard at times? Ask yourself do I really want to settle for shortcuts or live correcting my mistakes?

WEEK 23

MOTIVATIONAL MONDAY VITAMIN

(EXAMPLE)

It's imperative that we take time and count our blessings each day! All we must do is look around and see what's happening in the world with nonstop crime, disaster, disease, and misfortune. If you opened your eyes this morning and somehow stood on both feet, it was not by accident or surprise. You were destined to see another day, while a multitude of lives were cut short and unfortunately did not make it to this day. Think about that for a moment! Most people take life for granted as if they were supposed to wake up, able to see, hear, and move. However, the dichotomy is most people start recognizing the significant value of life once disaster hits home.

Therefore, we can't have it both ways. We either take life and precious moments for granted or we don't! We take value in getting up despite our failures of yesterday, or we use the unfortunate circumstances to determine our perspective on life. No matter what direction you end up, the pending result will be based off influence.

Today's motivational Monday vitamin is *example,* which is defined as a general rule to follow or imitate. Do you naturally lead by example or like to be made of an example? If you usually take the initiative to do things like taking out the trash, washing dirty dishes, completing errands, laundry, paying bills, and having pep talks with the children, you're a natural-born leader! Not only are you a natural-born leader, but one who leads by example. Some would argue that's not leading by example because it's their natural responsibility to do those things despite who's looking. However, we can't pretend like no one is watching or who is being impacted by our decisions. If no one else, our kids and spouses are paying attention whether we realize it or not.

Whether good or bad, you set the tone for which kind of example you want to be in life! If we're constantly making decisions that will ultimately cost our reputation, then we're leaving a bad example for those looking up to us. If we put ourselves in position to take care of responsibilities daily, we're leading by example for those who are irresponsible and lack understanding. How are you going to depend on your subordinate to do something you never showed them?

Bottom line, always remind yourself to be better today than you were yesterday. Realize while we will never be perfect, we never stop striving to perfect our God given talent and gifts. If you started a business, you don't give up on it when it's not meeting expectation. You stay with it until it begins to flourish and reach its' peak! Most successful people lead by example via hard work, earned money, and dedication they put into their business. Don't be labeled a dead-beat dad or mom by not raising that child the right way if circumstances change. Be the difference and show that you're not only willing to lead by example, but ultimately be the example!

WEEK 24

MOTIVATIONAL MONDAY VITAMIN

(SIGNIFICANCE)

Never say never! You were born for this moment! It's time to shine! Whatever the cliché, realize the relevance behind it. It may not be my time or your time, but it sure is go time! You ever feel like you blew it for the last time? How about the weight of the world on your shoulders? Do you feel like life is sometimes passing you by with only so many missed opportunities? Understand it's never over until it's over! If you are a part of humanity, flaws and imperfection is the name of the game. However, there is so much more than our inadequacies and short-comings as human beings.

Today's motivational Monday vitamin is *significance,* which is relative to importance or a quality of having a great worth! How do you measure up as a mere human being before any title is added to you? Does your level of self-worth come from your status at work? Is the amount of money you make shaping your character or corrupting good morals? No matter how difficult life becomes, we need to shift our focus to what we embody the most, significance! Figuratively, the world could not go round without each other working together!

Never be deceived with the world's philosophy telling you things like you're too small, or too slow, you will never make it to the pros! Young lady or man, you don't have it yet. You must accumulate this or do that to make this sizable amount. Do you think you have to look and think a certain way to feel a level of significance? Instead of feeling inadequate about your job position or wherever you stand in life, your purpose begins when realizing you have significance in that spot. Imagine if you suddenly didn't show up to work or failed to make your child's game. If the job struggles to fill in your spot or if your child missed expectation of seeing you, now do you see the significance involved?

Bottom line, recognize your significance first as a person. Second, realize the only person that can limit you is you! Third, allow your significance to impact the world around you by simply doing your job! There are always folk or someone depending on you. Therefore, step up to the plate, roll up your sleeves, put your hard hat on and stay the course. Every decision and move you make matters! When you fail, feeling like a spectator on sideline, understand your significance will get you back on course. If nothing else, understand you're just as important as the next person and you matter despite your physical appearance, intelligence, and age!

WEEK 

MOTIVATIONAL MONDAY VITAMIN

(RESPONSIBILITY)

You ever have an "oops" moment? You just spent a good 15-20 minutes preparing that last piece of turkey bacon for breakfast after cooking scrambled eggs and boom, it falls on the floor when you least expect it! Immediately your mind starts going places as you begin uttering words under your breath that is only common to man! We think to ourselves, "why did that just happened?" God must have a sense of humor for my last piece of bacon to hit the ground, knowing I don't do the three-second rule! It really makes you think, "well maybe it was not meant for me to have for my own good." "Had I eaten it, would it have gotten me sick?"

How about being so hungry that you ate very fast or snacked on something before encountering someone face to face? The problem is unconsciously, you forgot to check in the mirror to wipe the crumbs hanging from beard or corner of mouth. The person you encounter has a choice to acknowledge your appearance and say something about it to you or they can choose to ignore it, thinking it may cause further embarrassment.

Again, our first initial reaction to these "oops" moments is immediately going into "flight or fight" mode. In other words, we become fearful and begin rationalizing our feelings based on what just happened or we become defensive while instantly protecting ourselves. More than half of the oops moments can be avoided if we're a little extra careful and flat out responsible in our actions. Even dogs have a responsibility to bark during flight or fight!

Today's Motivational Monday vitamin is *responsibility,* which means the state or fact of being accountable, answerable, responsible for something within one's power, control, or management. It means the opportunity or ability to act independently and make decisions without authorization. We all have responsibility to some degree in simply doing our job as parents, children, students, workers, etc. It's second nature to wake up and take care of our hygiene before getting dressed and ready for the day. That's called responsibility. Are you responsible for feeding your small children and pets in the household? Are you responsible cleaning up behind yourself or running errands? How about paying bills or saving up money? Most of us heard the saying "to much is given, much is required." We want more accolades, but if the truth is told, we really don't want all the responsibilities that come along with it. Hip hop moguls, P-Diddy and Mase sung a lyric "Mo money, Mo problems… The more money we come around, the more problems we see."

So, no matter how much money you have, even the wealthy realize it's never enough. Every single one of us need to take responsibility for what we do daily. Remember bills won't pay itself, pets can't walk alone! Always be in position to take care of responsibility.

WEEK 26

MOTIVATIONAL MONDAY VITAMIN

(GRATITUDE)

How many times we say to ourselves "Man, I could've done that better," or "why did I just say that?" No matter what the issue is, we are our own biggest critic! Some people are perfectionists while others I dare to say, are apologists. Some are innovators and early adopters while others are late bloomers. No matter where you stand, there's always leeway for growth. Otherwise, we learn from our mistakes and try a new approach the next time we face a similar situation or find ourselves in a conundrum. There must be a wholesome approach to avoid self-criticism and having a sense of gratitude!

Today's Motivational Monday vitamin is *gratitude,* which is the quality of being thankful and focusing on what's good in our lives. According to Google, gratitude is pausing to notice and appreciate the things we often take for granted, like having food, a place to live, clean water, friends, family, etc. We must take advantage of the moment at hand! Time is never on our side. It's always running out. Therefore, we only pause to reflect and move forward to accept what life has to offer. We can either wallow in our self-pity or can be thankful for life despite our circumstances. Look around at the current events happening, assess the moment, be appreciative, and never have a short-term memory of how far you've come.

The journey in life is long. Some would even say it's a marathon race and not a sprint to the finish line. If you woke up this morning knowing you have a job to attend, be thankful. If you have a car to ride in or transportation money to get around, express your appreciation. If you went to tap mac or withdraw funds and somehow the money was available, have gratitude! Remember, some people are 5-10x worse than you are! While you woke up with all your limbs, there were millions struggling to use prosthetic aids. A lot of us woke up with all our sensory glands in place, able to see, hear, smell, and touch. There are people who wish they can see their loved ones, smell food or flowers, hear sound, or feel a loving touch.

Bottom line, we need to understand that whatever we're going through is beyond us. The only thing we can control is our decision to be nice or rude to people. We all heard the sayings "what comes around, goes around!" "You lay in the bed you've made." "You fall in the pit you dig for others." Even the "golden rule," "do unto others as you have them do unto you." The fact of the matter is most of us are facing adversity or circumstances to a degree. It's very easy to isolate ourselves from the world when our backs are up against the wall. It's difficult to continue in high spirits around others when it feels like you're the "dark horse." We must eradicate our feelings to think logically when facing hard times. Remember gratitude can take us very far in life if we can simply consider the things that matter.

MOTIVATIONAL MONDAY VITAMIN

(REPUTATION)

When you woke up this morning, how did you did feel? Better yet, when you laid down last night, what was your final thought before going to bed? If you could answer that question without hesitation, you're truly a sharp thinker! You're probably one most people would epitomize as the literal "pink elephant" in the room with that kind of memory. The fact of the matter is most of us can't remember what we thought or felt a half hour ago, much less last night or early this morning when waking up. However, if you're that one that can recite what you felt, thought, and said verbatim in chronological order, there's no doubt you're gifted!

Listen, you can have all the talents, accolades, money in the world and be the most gifted individual on God's green earth. It doesn't mean anything unless you have good character that can keep you where you can't afford to stay! Think of the legendary multi Grammy-award winner and phenomenal actor, Will Smith who literally made history in Hollywood. It seems like it all came crashing down during the 2022 Oscars Golden Globe Awards when he slapped his co-fellow mate, Chris Rock on stage in front of the world. We were all shocked and wondered what just happened. Was it staged? Why would Chris Rock joke about something so sensitive and personal to his peers in the academy? Whatever the rhyme or reason, this incident taught most of us that you will be remembered most by your character and reputation!

Today's Motivational Monday vitamin is *reputation,* which means the opinion that people in general have about someone or something. It's a widespread belief that someone or something has a particular habit or characteristic. Again, you can have all the money, intelligence, fame, and power in the world. At the end of the day, all you really have is your name with a number attached to you. By the way, the number I speak of is not your net worth, but your social security number. There are plenty of people in general and celebrities that make mistakes all the time, even causing them to fall from grace. Just a few years ago, the sexual allegations of accused executive producers, actors, and analysts made headlines all throughout Hollywood and national media platforms. Today, we see athletic stars and celebrities speaking their mind on sensitive cultural views, costing their reputation.

No matter how good you are at something with the influence you share with the world, it could all be lost in in an instant by decisions you make. Everything in our modern day is about being "politically correct." Therefore, if you have a strong belief about a certain group of people or thing, it's best to keep it to yourself rather than sharing with the world. Remember, some people will remember you more for that one bad choice, tarnishing your reputation rather than all the good you brought about. Bottom line, leave a legacy for a good reputation oppose to a bad one so that when you're gone from this life and people mention your name, it's good vibes!

WEEK 28

MOTIVATIONAL MONDAY VITAMIN

(FOCUS)

You ever ponder on thoughts of where life is taking you or leading to? You may be going through a circumstance affecting your health, finances, family, career, relationships, etc. You may have just blown a big business deal, lost a job, or something very valuable. We feel helpless and vulnerable the most when we lose control and the sky is falling. You know the "woe is me" feeling. We react based on the outcome of our situation. If the risk outweighs the reward, most of us will take the safer approach by limiting our chances at something. On the contrary, if the reward outweighs the risk, chances are we take more chances! However, in order to make a decision for taking more or less chances, we have to be disciplined with focus.

Today's Motivational Monday vitamin is *focus,* which means center of activity, attraction, or attention. It is the act of concentrating interest or activity on something. The focus should never be keeping eyes in the rear view mirror while driving. Our focus needs to be straight ahead in direction of where we're going instead of what's behind us. Drivers occasionally peak through rear mirror while primarily keeping focus ahead for safety purpose during the course of driving. Stop focusing on who offended or hurt you in past and look forward to how you can begin healing process!

If you're that one who keep focusing on past failures or accomplishments, you're more than likely setting yourself up for a rude awakening. In other words, you don't know the uncertainties that lie ahead like potential barriers, pedestrians, or simple detours due to road closures. Learn to let go of what happened yesterday or a few years ago and shift focus to what's coming next. Notice I did not say what's happening now. We can't change our past by erasing mistakes and rewinding the hands of time. However, we can change our future by not repeating same mistakes. We all know the definition of insanity is doing the same thing over and over again, and expecting different results!

Bottom line, our focus needs to be so sharp, that distractions and getting side-tracked become foreign to us. To focus means minimizing distractions and maximizing your undivided attention. How many times we try giving our focus to something like a meeting, our kids or loved ones discussing a problem, health concerns, etc.? All of a sudden, we're distracted with a call or text message on our phone, a highlight on television, or we start thinking about the time for our regular routine schedule. Remember to always focus on God for better faith, self for bigger confidence, and family for rewarding love and relationship.

WEEK 29

MOTIVATIONAL MONDAY VITAMIN

(RECHARGE)

We hear it all the time especially in professional sports, how "speed kills." We absolutely love pro-athletes who performs at the highest level, leaving their opponents in the dust. It's almost unfair to teams and opponents who are up against the Tyreek Hills and Usain Bolts of the world. Who doesn't like speed? There might be some who oppose speed and lean more toward the old school tradition of conservatism. Yes, I would beg the differ that there are those who prefer slowing things down due to the fast pace reaction involved. However, we're living in a day and time where just about everything we face requires speed. Think about it! Our internet most of us live off on a daily basis demands speed to work properly. If the truth is told, most people will admit they're over the speed limit trying to get to their place of destination. We throw the pile of nasty dishes in dishwasher, food in air fryers, or microwave for speeding up the process. Prime members like myself order on Amazon with the expectation of receiving delivered items the following day or within few days oppose to weeks. We as well as our devices run on speed every day and require a certain amount of rest to continue the cycle.

Therefore, in order to constantly run on speed, we need to recharge. Today's Motivational Monday vitamin is *recharge,* which means to restore, renew, or charge again. It's similar to recharging a battery or a smart phone. Think of yourself as that battery or device that requires charging. In most cases, analytics on our smart devices such as phones, tablets, watches, or even laptops will give an indicator to recharge when battery is running low. How do you sense the indicator to recharge when constantly on go-mode throughout week? Are you listening to the indicator once identifying what it is? It's one thing to sense the indicator or signals our bodies are telling us, and it's another when actually responding while doing something about it.

We never have a problem with remembering to carry our device chargers when going somewhere for an extended period of time. The same should apply for our mind, body, and soul! Teachers who teach k-12 can absolutely feel exhausted at the end of day because young children and teenagers can zap you of your strength. The same applies to stay-at-home moms raising little ones! Transportation, truckers, and share drive workers are tired due to the long hours of driving around town.

Whatever your profession, whether it's changing diapers or changing tires, it will demand a level of recharging. You might ask what does this recharging look like? It may be simple rest, taking a vacation, workout routine, re-igniting faith, eating, or prayer/ meditation. Always be of the mindset to recharge before running out of energy and remember, you can't give your hundred percent if you're not charged a hundred percent.

MOTIVATIONAL MONDAY VITAMIN

(INITIATIVE)

Imagine walking down the street in your local neighborhood and suddenly out the clear blue sky, you're met eye to eye with a ferocious mountain lion. You got only two choices, run for your life or stand there hoping and even praying God grant you a miracle like he did with Daniel in the lion's den. What are the chances you get eaten by that mountain lion by taking off with all the adrenaline in you versus a stare down match with fierceness in your eyes? Believe it or not, according to scientific American study, the Dept. of fish and game warns to not run when confronting big cats and other similar wildlife.

The study further indicates a slighter higher percentage of people dying from attacks when running versus lower percentage of those who survived while remaining motionless. One would think, "either way, I'm done no matter what decision I make." However, the study indicated an even higher percentage of survival or not being attacked at all for those who slowly backed away from the deadly animal oppose to running out of fear. Understand predators can sense fear from their prey. So when in doubt, have enough faith to trust yourself. Instead of being so afraid, learn to look your opponent in the eye with courage so you don't fall prey to your greatest fear! The only way to take on this challenge is taking the initiative.

Today's motivational Monday vitamin is *initiative,* which means the ability to judge what needs to be done and take action without suggestion of other people. It's the ability to assess and initiate things independently. Therefore, going back to our story of facing the mountain lion. You can take the initiative to flat out run or be still while slowly backing away. The real question to you is what are you doing about the mountain lion you're facing? It could be a mountain load of debt. It could be a life-threatening health concern. It could be a bad relationship or trouble with the law. You see no matter what transpired, it's up to us to take the initiative of "where do we go from here." How do I get rid of this debt versus worrying about it? What's the plan of punching back when getting punched too much? Taking the initiative means taking on the role of a leader and not sitting on hands.

Therefore, as you challenge yourself this week to face that mountain lion square in the eye, take the initiative to react in survival mode oppose to giving yourself up for the death penalty. In other words, don't run from your problems. Face them and begin doing something about it rather than nothing at all. If you started that business, continue it until you begin seeing results. If you're facing eviction or bankruptcy, talk with someone to help financially. Take the initiative!

MOTIVATIONAL MONDAY VITAMIN

(CREDIBILITY)

Most people are searching for happiness, a sense of purpose, and even balance. We all love a good laugh as "laughter is good for the soul." However, we also understand sometimes circumstances happen and get the best of us at times. What happens when our backs are against the wall? Bills are on override! Our dependents constantly remind us how expensive they are as the money is looking funny. For some, sickness and disease begins to settle in. The list goes on regarding adversity and the eves and flows of our circumstances! We think to ourselves if I only had this or if only things were different, working in my favor! Here comes the good news! Do more of what you love so that there's no room for despair! Have a heart of empathy oppose to growing cold and callous towards people. Do more giving than receiving and taking. Show more character rather than corruption. These attributes only happen with good intentions & true authenticity.

Today's Motivational Monday vitamin is *credibility.* It is the quality of being trusted and believed in. Credibility holds the connotation of convincing or being believable. Picture it as the badge on an officer, a wedding ring on your finger, or similar genes in your child. In other words, it is a symbolic indicator stating "I'm who they say I'm." It's officially real, one hundred percent, and authentic. There's no grey area, no fake news, or cutting around corners with credibility. You either have it or you don't have it. Most of us will buy from a source we trust primarily due to its' credibility. Amazon Prime members like myself will purchase items again and again on the official website store because it's a trusted source and the convenience behind it. We usually go to same hair stylist for many years due to the relationship and trust factor in knowing what we plan to get done during each appointment.

Credibility goes beyond me or you! It's bigger than what you might perceive it to be. We as parents have to be so trustworthy, that our children no matter how old they get, can see our trustworthiness. We can't live a certain lifestyle in the eyes of our children and then turn around tell them not to live the same way. We know that's hypocritical and contradictive. We as grown-ups have to know better and quite frankly, do better! Dads, let's step up our game with our sons & daughters, raising them the right way and showing them what a true man resembles. Sometimes, it will require apologizing for some things we caused in the past and getting it right. Moms, while full of so much love and nurture for your children, it's important to set boundaries of parenting over bonding so the respect is not lost. Remember to always show credibility to gain the trust of others no matter what you say, do, or represent. It's bigger than us!

WEEK 32

MOTIVATIONAL MONDAY VITAMIN
(HEALTH)

Most people around the holidays inevitably take time off from work, go on a mini vacation, or simply have a staycation at home to get more done. For some, work is an everyday livelihood, while it's a burden to others. You either love what you do or don't. In some cases, you find purpose in what you do and begin to develop a love for it! If you're not happy at this point in your career, take the next step in moving on. We know it's easier said than done. However, we only reach our ceiling by first jumping off the floor. Take advantage of each opportunity and seize the moment. If you're educated and smart, you will never sell yourself short to an any employer counter-offering your requested expectation! In other words, you know that you have what it takes to effectively and proficiently perform the job duties at the highest level for negotiable salary & benefits. Whether you love what you do or looking just to make money by any means of work, you need to be in good mental & physical shape!

Today's Motivational Monday vitamin is *health,* which is the state of being free from illness or injury. It's a person's complete mental or physical condition. It's imperative to have good health so that you can be at your best performance! If work requires a physical demand, your health plays a vital role in effectively completing job duties. I have personally learned even as a certified fitness advocate, we can eat all the right foods, take our vitamins/supplements, exercise daily and still become sick with the common cold, flu, injuries, etc. Sickness is a part of life. We can't escape it or control it. However, we can mitigate symptoms or life-threatening diseases by watching our diet, minimizing substance abuse, exercising, wash hands often, use protective barriers, take prescribed medication, and following up with doctors as necessary.

Let us remind ourselves as we go throughout this week to be so ever vigilant about our health. Without it, life becomes miserable and frustrating. Think of your health as the very breath you breathe through your lungs. When that breath is cut off or short, you begin to suffocate. No one wants to suffocate their life away. Sometimes circumstances get the best of us and it feels like we might be suffocating. Learn to make right decisions in food choices, as it's so easy to munch down a fast food combo that we know is bad for our health but still do it. You are what you eat is true! You'll feel good when eating healthy and feel bad when making poor decisions. Our health is so essential that it can impact the entire world at large. Covid-19 put the nations at a major crisis with a lock down and financial woes we'll never forget. No more excuses! It's time to correctly diet, exercise, & protect ourselves in order to boost health and prevent chances of suffering from life-long chronic diseases.

WEEK 33

MOTIVATIONAL MONDAY VITAMIN

(STRENGTH)

How many times you forgot something after leaving out to work or a trip somewhere? You start to think to yourself "what's wrong with me?" or "Man! I'm getting old!" You wonder if you need a shot of B-12 or pure vitamin supplements for muscle memory. Bottom line, we all forget to do something because we all are human! We can relate to each other as people due to our fallible nature of making mistakes or simply being wrong at times. There are some who think of themselves as being self-righteous and above everyone else in a "perfect world." Also, there are those who are so inferior, that everything they tend to do, say, think, or feel is perceived as a mistake.

No matter the perception of how we look at ourselves, no one person is above another or beneath another on the human level. Take the titles and authority away from your position, while stripping your mind bare as a human being. What do you have left? You, the person is all you have left with equal rights and God-given ability like your neighbor next to you. Remember the next time you compare yourself with another person, realize they're human just like you and have areas of weakness that require strength.

Today's Motivational Monday vitamin is *strength,* which means the quality or state of being physically strong. It's the capacity of an object or substance to withstand great force or pressure. Imagine being in a tug-a-war with several huge muscular figures on one end, while you and a half dozen feather weight guys on the other. Common sense may tell us the huge muscular figures win the tug-a-war and win it quite candidly!

However, strength is in the details and those same huge muscular guys could very well lose the tug-a-war if their approach and strategy is not fitting. In other words, if these muscular figures don't attempt to use all their power, thinking they already won on paper due to their size advantage, they might be in for a rude awakening. You and the featherweight crew could possibly have a plan to win the tug-a-war by building on each other strength oppose to being fearful of perception.

As we go throughout this week, we need to draw on our inner strength of spirituality. Whatever that spirituality looks like, we need to affirm and grab hold of it for our own peace of mind! Some may pray and meditate, while others might dive into the essence of music, solitude, and literature. You might huddle with friends and family to express love. There are those who exercise self-care in working out on daily basis and meditating to reduce stress. You could find that inner strength of self-talk, where you're motivating yourself to do better. Remember, strength is not just physical. It is emotional, mental, and social as well. It always begins and ends in the mind. Mind over matter equals strength!

MOTIVATIONAL MONDAY VITAMIN

(EXTEND)

Reality tells us for every beginning there's an ending. Remember, it's not how you start, it's how you end. Think of the times you started something but never finished. What is blocking you from completing the task? It's only common that interruption is a part of the process when trying to finish a project such as writing a book, finishing school, creating a music label, obtaining licensure, saving to purchase that dream home, or successfully owning your business! The distractions we normally face are usually detractors that get us off our game plan. Whatever the end-goal we discussed in previous weeks has to become our reality! In spite of what you don't have, consider how good you have it in comparison to some who unfortunately doesn't have it so well.

Today's motivational Monday vitamin is *Extend,* which means to make longer, hold something out toward someone; exert or exercise oneself to the utmost. All we have to do is simply look around at our surroundings and realize how fortunate we are while others wish they could attain a portion of the pie! Think about the homeless on the street, where their next meal is coming from. How about the over representation of indigenous children being held against their will for commercial sex trafficking or labor coercion?

There are people confined to their beds, missing limbs, unable to talk or walk while we're planning the next upgrade on vehicles and more ways to find financial freedom to live the "*American Dream.*" We as Americans can freely walk down our neighborhood streets, hold up signs in protest while others in third world countries are literally in hiding due to fear of war and dictatorship. The next time you come across a person or group of individuals in need of help, remember to extend yourself for assistance.

As we go through this week, we need to remind ourselves about another whole world out there less fortunate than we are in every sense of the word. What's wrong with extending your hand to help someone who fell off the ground? I guess it's okay to be somewhat human and not live as if the world resolves around you. It's even better to extend human-kindness while bringing resolution to the world! People are suffering and we can make the difference by showing a good part of humanity despite the detractors. You never know what someone is going through until being in their shoes. Always make time to extend your assistance to people who need it most, starting with lending your time, effort, and resources.

MOTIVATIONAL MONDAY VITAMIN

(RESILIENCE)

Last night came and went. Today is a new day, full of new promises and grace! You get a clearer perspective when you view things in front of you oppose to focusing on the things behind you. It's time to walk in your purpose! It's time to shake off the excuses. The fact that you began reading this vitamin when there were a hundred other things going on, says you're locked and tuned in! I know you're asking yourself, what's next? What's the next turning point now that I accomplished this task? It could be putting the final pieces in place, getting one step closer in reaching the end-goal. We all have our magical moments when that dream we fantasized about over the years finally comes true! Some strike gold, hitting the lottery jackpot, while others get to see what it's like in another country on a dream trip. If we're going to experience that magical moment, whether greeting Mickey at Disney World, walking grown daughter down aisle on wedding day, or finally getting paid for something we absolutely love doing, it will require resilience.

Today's Motivation Monday vitamin is *resilience,* which means the capacity to recover quickly from difficulties; toughness or adversity standing in the way. It's the ability of a substance or thing to spring back into shape, elasticity. Imagine taking a piece of paper and balling it up before stepping on it over and over again. Now picture taking that same paper that had been stomped on, crumbled up, and left for waste somehow in your hand for the possibility of renewal. We know pure gold is made by going through a refinery process with the most unimaginable intensifying heat. Most things we crave like coffee, wine, grains, sugar, etc. requires a great deal of pressure and refinery to add value. How resilient are you when times get rough, when the rubber meets the road in the time of challenges?

Resilience tells us no matter what we're facing or going through when our backs are up against the wall, we can always bounce back! Clay in the hand of the potter could be made for a good purpose or a bad cause. It could be made into an eloquent, shiny dish or it can be mangled and left to rot. Only time will tell how that piece of clay bounces back oppose to being scooped up and thrown away. If that clay had any signs of workability, the potter will pick it up and put it to use until it officially fulfilled its' purpose of becoming what it was meant to be. We need to show signs of workability instead of rigidity or stiffness to be made into something beautiful! Resilience allows us to keep going with life when circumstances and different voices are telling us the opposite. Remember, the only way we get to see a new fresh start in fulfilling our purpose is resilience in the face of adversity!

MOTIVATIONAL MONDAY VITAMIN

(SOLUTION)

Are you conscious enough to sense a sudden change in atmosphere? We've all been there with a change of direction. You know, when our adrenaline is pumping, the heart begins pounding, and the norepinephrine is released for the "fight or flight" approach. We react based on what is happening in our surroundings. If a brawl breaks out in a local crowd, do you A- immediately pull out your phone and begin recording? B- run or call for help? C- join in the brawl because it somehow involves people you know? D- ignore it, none of my business? One thing for sure, someone will address each of those reactional responses in some form or fashion in today's world.

Today's Motivational Monday vitamin is *solution*- a means of solving a problem or dealing with a difficult situation. How many of us really like doing the dirty dishes in sink/unloading dishwasher, cleaning bathroom, paying bills, cutting grass, or doing laundry? I'll answer for you, none of us! We somehow manage to do these chores because it's our responsibility, unless we have Maid or Butler services in place. Think about car repair issues, parking/moving violations, and managing stress in the workplace. Have you considered for every action there's a reaction? Otherwise, we usually witness the outcome of our actions when faced with the decisions and choices we inevitably make.

Some of us serve and/or work with very difficult people on a daily basis. We hold pertinent positions in our field of practice that require quick solutions in little turnaround time! We may not have all the answers or problem-solving skills it takes for addressing the overwhelming number of problems we face. However, we do have this thing called "common sense," which solves a lot of issues in itself by making smart and wise decisions. You ever heard the infamous quote? "Don't be a part of the problem, be a part of the solution." It's really up to you and I to come up with a solution or find a way to be part of the resolution unless we become part of the problem. Remember, we may not be able to solve everyone's problems. We can certainly exercise our responsibility to complete the task and mitigate more problems by continually looking for a solution ahead!

MOTIVATIONAL MONDAY VITAMIN

(SELF-CARE)

We constantly have to remind ourselves to take breaks, take deep breaths, go for a walk, and do better! We're only human and bound to make mistakes no matter how hard we try to be perfect at something. Sometimes we find ourselves giving it our all, one hundred percent of the time. Think about your favorite star athlete that sacrifices his or her absolute best for the benefit of the team. That athlete usually gives their all until he or she begin pressing when competition is turned up a notch! When the pressure is on, usually mistakes begin happening. There are consecutive missed shots, passes, and even turnovers. Why? We start second-guessing ourselves, overthinking things when faced with competition and wanting to be confident at something despite the surrounding support.

Today's Motivational Monday vitamin is *self-care*, which is the process of establishing behaviors to ensure holistic well-being of oneself, to promote health, and actively manage illness as it occurs. How many times have you heard "self-care is the best the care," or "how can you care for others when you can't care for yourself?" Self-care means you're providing care for yourself, not fifty other people. It doesn't mean you're selfish, or don't care about others. It's simply a lifestyle decision you make so that you can effectively care for others! When was the last time you treated yourself to something you really enjoy? Is it too much to ask of yourself to do more of what makes you happy?

Remember to exercise self-care without feeling any guilt! We have to remind ourselves that it's okay to take a vacation or break away from work. It's absolutely fine to go shopping for clothes when most of our money is spent on bills and big-head kids who constantly have their hand out! It's nothing wrong with going to barbershop, hair & nail salon, movies, place of worship, or even doctor office. Otherwise, stress weighs on us to the point where sickness becomes a reality. We do know misery loves company! We need to go throughout this week with the mindset of having grace on ourselves instead of being our own worst critic!

MOTIVATIONAL MONDAY VITAMIN

(PERSPECTIVE)

How many times have you heard someone say "never take life for granted?" If you're old enough, you probably heard it a ton of times. Why do you think mostly older folk will embed that mantra in your head time and time again? So much can happen instantaneously as life could change on you in a bat of an eye! We might think we got time to do this and do that in our strategic planning for accomplishing goals while setting trends. However, reality tells us life circumstances and bumps in the road do happen as things don't always pan out the way we anticipate from the beginning. We often hear people say "I got to keep myself in check." Ultimately, what their saying is there need to be more discipline in their self-control.

Today's Motivational Monday vitamin is *perspective,* which is a mental view or prospect; a visible scene. It's how you're seeing things from your point of view. We all know it's good to have different perspectives pertaining to analytical data on our health, finances, job creation, education, and mental well-being. We heard people formulate questions, asking what is your perspective on this? Do we need to gain a different perspective? Did you try looking at it from their perspective instead of your own? Perspective plays a huge part in our mental well-being and it's certainly up to us to define how we put it into practice.

Everyone has a perspective. It's how you use the perspective that determines the outcome of your perception! The reality of us having bills and debt to pay gives the perception of never-ending financial woes and focus on responsibility. If our perspective remains the same, more than likely our circumstances remain the same. Sometimes we have to change our perspective to clearly see what's happening and why.

Never be bias because someone else share the same perspective as you. It's not always a bad thing to look through the lenses of different glasses, especially if you have difficulty seeing out your own! Let your perspective carry you over the hump day this week. Always be open to different point of views and do not allow your perspective to inevitably outweigh the perspective of others. If we allow ourselves to feed off one another during the biggest teaching moments, we can actually learn something new oppose to being set in our ways, focused on own perspective!

MOTIVATIONAL MONDAY VITAMIN

(STABILITY)

How many weeks will it take to finally realize you got this? You learned how to tie your shoes, ride on training wheels, write a check, apply for a job, and achieve driver's license for the first time! Now you understand since being pushed, it comes a time to push yourself. It's called utilizing your *independence!* We naturally exercise independence since childhood development such as walking, talking, and thinking. The psychology behind our independence is all about taking what we've learned and applying it to our everyday lives.

Today's Motivational Monday vitamin is *stability,* which is the quality or degree of being stable. It's literally the strength to stand or endure; firmness. Whenever there's inquiry about something or someone having stability, it usually involves a source seeking longevity for its' intended purpose! In other words, does this person or business truly have what it takes to make ends meet or get us over the top? If there's any signs or hint of weakness that this source might crumble before reaching the top, then all bets are off. Stability teaches us the solid wisdom of advancing ahead while so much failure is prevalent surrounding our circumstances.

We look for ways to escape reality, especially when our backs are against the wall and the grey skies are falling. There are some that would rather live their lives in virtual reality, caught up in gaming apps, computers, online communities to somehow mitigate the stress of real life circumstances. However, we need to remind ourselves that you can't form the word "*stability*" without acknowledging the word "*ability.*" Stability says we need to have ability whether learned activity or independently influenced to arise to the pinnacle of our success! Don't allow any fear of the unknown to dictate your future of stability!

WEEK 40

MOTIVATIONAL MONDAY VITAMIN

(WIN)

The last thing we want to do is put all our eggs in one basket, hoping somehow it meets the desired expectations we tend to focus on. We never want to get to a point where we're scrambling after loose change on the ground. In other words, it's best to keep our head on a swivel and stay focused oppose to being distracted by the smallest of circumstances surrounding us! The easy thing is quitting, giving up, throwing in the towel, or going into flight instead fight mode when our backs are against the wall. It takes a great deal of resiliency and fortitude to withstand the battle we're up against.

Today's Motivational Monday vitamin is *win,* a successful result in a contest, conflict, bet, or other endeavor; victory. You ever hear anyone say "all I want is a win," or "we're winning?" Most of us know the famous quote by the late great Al Davis- "Just win baby!" Winning has a lot to do with culture, core values, and a strong volition of achievement. You ever notice some sport teams that have a winning culture over others that tend to have a losing culture? In sports, is winning more about culture, talent, discipline, coaching, or all the above?

If someone cuts you off on the road or hit your car, your natural response is possibly reacting on how you feel in the moment. The question becomes do you celebrate with a win when cutting that person off, giving the bird, or simply humiliating them all across social media in retaliation? Is that a winning mentality or loser remorse? News flash, we can't really win if we're contributing to others losing. You see, we really lose when we stop others from winning, and we win when getting rid of a loser's mentality!

Bottom line, we need to remind ourselves there are different ways to win. Think of your favorite star athletes, whether they're professional or your very own in little leagues. The last thing we want to see is a big-time star shrinking in the biggest of moments. Remember to win, it will require a great deal of preparation, ethos, and discipline. If there are 7 days with 168 total hours in a week, how many of those days with allotted amount of time are you experiencing wins over defeats? Make sure to do the things that will outsmart your opponents. It's a game of chess and not checkers! Always strive to win!

MOTIVATIONAL MONDAY VITAMIN

(INSPIRE)

This week might be full of plenty of surprises whether good or bad! Only time will tell how you end up on the other side of that particular situation. You might've just found out some concerning news about your health as your heart began pacing and anxiety antennas rose up. Maybe your teenage child, significant other, or close friend just revealed they are in an abusive relationship and have nowhere to turn but you! How about taking that board state exam after countless hours of preparation with unsettled feelings of confidence or inadequacy? Surprisingly, you found out that not only did you pass, but with flying colors! No matter what, our human emotional intelligence tells us we need to take the good with the bad despite the surprising results of uncontrollable situations.

Today's Motivational Monday vitamin is *inspire,* which means to fill someone with the urge or ability to do or feel something. It also means to create a positive feeling in someone. We often hear "You inspire me to do more," "You're my greatest inspiration," or "always inspire to be great!" There are a ton of inspirational quotes that we gravitate to or feel motivated to live by the standard or weight it holds. Quotes like "don't be pushed around by the fears in your mind. Be led by the dreams in your heart," -Roy T. Bennett. "You've gotta dance like there's nobody watching, love like you'll never be hurt, sing like there's nobody listening, and live like it's heaven on earth." –William W. Purkey. "Be the change that you wish to see in the world." –Mahatma Gandhi. "Always strive for more. Never settle for anything less." – general.

Not only do inspirational quotes get our juices flowing; it's more in what a person does with setting a golden standard to live by! We're impacted or influenced by the way people carry out their business. It might be a dear loved one who maintains a safe, clean, organized living environment so much so, that it rubs off on you. How about that family member who takes time out to seek the delicate needs and support for everyone, stepping up as a servant-leader? Maybe it's the loved one or individual who chose success over being ordinary or settling for mediocracy. It could be your favorite actor/actress, TV host, best author, pro-athlete, spiritual leader, military veteran, or even political figure who all contributes to the inspiration you desire to obtain!

We all have the ability to create the change and be the change so that we can inspire others to do the same! Always look for ways to inspire others by taking what you do well and excelling at it. You never know what kind of impact you might have on someone by being authentic in your benefit to others. Remember, you don't necessarily need to have a lot of money, fame, prestige, or power to inspire. It will require to live above average, be a little extraordinary, and being approachable. Who or what inspires you? By the time you reach the why, you'll understand a little more of what it takes to inspire others in your own unique way. Learn to be inspired so that you can take what you know and inspire others!

ABOUT THE AUTHOR

This author has found a passionate love for art, fitness & health, and writing for inspirational purpose. He is very creative in tapping into the human emotional intelligence of people from all walks of life! The author holds weight in the creativity of understanding people with a thorough strong background in social services over the past 20 years. He has a natural born instinct for being inspirational by always encouraging, empowering, and motivating others to bring forth their best effort and becoming the best version of themselves. He is all about making a huge impact in the small ways of changing the lives of people by exercising his gift of exhortation. Furthermore, he loves a lifestyle that mingles with joy, happiness, humour, adventure, and challenge among family and friends outside the profession of making a difference in people lives.

Printed in the United States
by Baker & Taylor Publisher Services